FACILITY MANAGEMENT OUTSOURCING RELATIONSHIP

KA LEUNG LOK & DAVID BALDRY

Contents

Preface

Abstract Purpose – This paper aims to test the nine corollaries concerning the determinants of outsourcing relationship dimensions, strategic manoeuvres, clients' and service providers' evaluation regarding outsourcing category and outsourcing relationship types. The paper has the purpose of reviewing the concept of outsourcing in relation to FM, dealing with service providers' performance and its effect on clients before providing a comprehensive discussion of outsourcing. Design/methodology/approach – A conceptual approach is adopted, suggesting that a study of outsourcing relationship between clients and service providers from these theoretical perspectives is used to develop corollaries about the relationships between the strategic manoeuvres identified and the different dimensions of outsourcing relationship. The corollaries are examined using non-parametric tests.

Findings – The model of the facilities management (FM) outsourcing relationships presented in the paper shows performance of outsourcing services through evaluation of outsourcing categories on current and future FM contracts of clients and service providers. As a template of outsourcing relationships, the model is the context for predicting the important outsourcing categories to the future four FM outsourcing contracts, such as building maintenance, security, cleaning and catering. On prediction of those FM contracts, there is an inclination to the types of in-house and technical expertise on category of FM outsourcing relationship types from clients, whilst there is an equal inclination to the type of in-house outsourcing category from service providers. Originality/value – Management on outsourcing relationships between clients and service providers is now essential for effective outsourcing in FM. This paper provides an intriguing insight into how the effect of outsourcing relationships can be strategically implemented into the performance of service providers.

Acknowledgements

First Author

Dr. Ka Leung Lok (Lawrence)

Academically, Lawrence was awarded his PhD from School of Built Environment of University of Salford. He got his B. Sc. (Honour) Degree in Building from The City University of Hong Kong and MBA in Construction and Real Estate from The University of Reading. Professionally, Lawrence is developing as a consultant, lecturer and manager in the field of construction and real estate. His research interests are in the areas of Facilities Management Outsourcing relationships and relevant ISO series.

Prologue

Table of content

CHAPTER ONE

Introduction of facility management outsourcing strategy

Although the construction industry has long been a powerful engine for Hong
Kong's economic growth, the industry experienced a drastic reduction in
workloads and a change in market structure following the Asian economic
turmoil in 1997 (Chiang et al., 2013). Consequently, regional FM outsourcing
services for built environments have grown more common. These outsourcing
services include computer integrated FM, catering/vending, moving
management, project management (for both major and minor works), services
installation (i.e., mechanical, electrical) and cleaning or security services
(Moore and Finch, 2004). In the late 1990s in Hong Kong, expenditures for in-
house services became a greater burden with the drop in rental incomes, and
building owners outsourced many of these services (Lai, Yik and Jones, 2008;
Yik and Lai, 2005). To decrease their costs, many commercial building owners
chose to outsource operations and maintenance work, according to the results

of their feasibility studies. The Tertiary Education Facilities Management Association (2011) reports that more than 50% of its benchmark data are found in the facilities management services at the seven universities in Hong
Kong, including energy consumption, maintenance services, refurbishments
and building operating costs, and especially the costs of security services, cleaning and waste management services.

Kok, et al. (2011) find that cleaning and maintenance services have a major
and direct effect on students' academic achievement, and that catering and security services can affect staff and student satisfaction and the
organisation's image. These four facility services can each add specific values
to the higher education sector. This study thus focuses on the four FM outsourcing services of maintenance, cleaning, security and catering, as they
are supplied in Hong Kong's higher education sector.

Before discussing client and service provider relationships or the nature of
their operational and management elements, it is important to distinguish between the two terms of 'contracting-out' and 'outsourcing'. 'Contracting-out'
normally refers to those services that continue to be provided in-house but have been directly contracted, whereas 'outsourcing' refers to services that continue to be procured from external providers.

The purpose of this study is to investigate the outsourcing relationships between the clients and service providers in a key sector of Hong Kong's economy. Fully understanding these outsourcing relationships requires taking
a holistic view of the fundamental elements of outsourcing, including the nature, services, strategies and the management of relationships. Such an understanding also involves examining these elements within appropriate theoretical models. The literature reveals the general working mechanisms of
outsourcing (Boer et al., 2006; Maskell et al., 2005), but the significance of this study lies in its explication of the previously obscure relationships between FM outsourcing service providers and their clients.

In recent decades, integrated resource planning (the main resources being
people, property and technology) has become an important part of FM. It is generally believed that the optimal use of high-quality facilities can solve business problems in the built and human environment. To operate such facilities, outsourcing is now prevalent in various industries. This procurement
approach is considered by some proponents to be an effective and efficient approach to managing resources (Adegoke and Adegoke, 2013; Agndal and Nordin, 2009; Hamzah et al., 2010; Ikediashi et al. 2013; Kadefors, 2008; Li and Choi, 2009). However, organisations often fail to consider how the performance of the outsourced service providers affects their business success. It is also often unclear how the type of outsourcing relationship affects business success. Developing a specific outsourcing model is therefore highly useful to the FM industry.

In summary, there are several reasons behind choosing Hong Kong's higher
education sector for this study. The sector is one of the most active and sophisticated, best developed and most up-to-date economic sectors. Also, this sector has recently played a highly significant role in Hong Kong. Finally,
the local higher education sector has a large economic base with strong competition between universities and institutes. The selected universities and
tertiary institutes have similar varieties of FM services, which are offered by different service providers in other institutes. This study thus strongly emphasises FM outsourcing strategies within various contracts, which is one
of the variables of the model. Specific FM outsourcing contracts for catering,
cleaning, security and maintenance are selected for examination.

CHAPTER TWO

Study FM outsource goals

This study investigates the performance of outsourcing service providers.
l It aims to establish a clear link between FM performance and business performance.
l It aims to gain better understanding on the development of outsourcing relationships between clients and service providers during their contractual periods.

Why this study is needed

l The service providers expect to enhance their own capability in the formulation of outsourcing strategies.
l The service providers expect to provide better outsourcing services to their clients by improving their own analytical, managerial, cooperative and professional skills in solving their relationship management problems.
l The clients expect to gain understanding on how to select the optimum service providers for their specific FM outsourcing contractual procurement needs.
l The clients expect to maximise value for their money in each FM outsourcing contract through improved effectiveness.

Currently, organisations are required to reduce costs in a competitive environment, and the education institutions in Hong Kong are no exception.
They need to have balanced budgets, and they can cut costs by outsourcing. The importance of FM as a means of encouraging learning has been emphasised by the majority of higher-education-related FM studies (Amaratunga and Baldry, 1999; Price et al., 2003; Fianchini, 2006; Lavy, 2008). Vidalakis et al. (2013) also indicate the potential of facilities management and maintenance services to create value, especially for higher education institutions. Such value creation can potentially be greater than

that
created by the construction of new high-profile facilities. The organisations
can improve their revenue by increasing user satisfaction with FM services,
thus attracting more students. This study proposes that outsourcing
manoeuvres can affect the types and the quality of outsourcing
relationships,
and thus affect profits.

In summary, clients; satisfaction depends on service providers' services.
After
understanding the minds of their clients, the service providers can tailor-
make
their own business strategies for sustainable development. Thus, the
purpose
of this study is not only to examine the performance of the service
providers,
but also and more crucially, to understand the standards of service that their
clients expect, now and in the future. It is expected that the clients'
demands
can be fulfilled through the service providers' efforts. To enable this,
however,
it is important to discover the optimal outsourcing relationships between
clients and service providers through understanding the links between
outsourcing relationship dimensions and manoeuvres.

CHAPTER THREE

Outsourcing in Facilities Management

Insights into the future of outsourcing

Sia et al. (2008) state that outsourcing is now a strategic option that few organisations can afford to ignore. The current major trend in outsourcing is

towards smaller and more strategic deals – the kinds that reflect businesses' strategies for realising their goals and objectives. Clients make sustainable savings by focusing on measures of end-to-end process efficiency. Service providers provide the industry insights, geographical diversity, technical innovations and high-value skills necessary to enter new markets and exploit

opportunities (IAOP, 2012). In the near future, there are many directions in which outsourcing research can be taken. It seems that the broad underlying managerial interest is to gain a greater understanding of the factors responsible for the success of outsourcing (Hätönen and Eriksson, 2009; Ikediashi et al. 2012 and 2013). Adegoke and Adegoke (2013) find that outsourcing reduces risk due to reliance on experts and infusion on new technology in tertiary institutions. Correctly managing the outsourcing process

is vital to ensure positive outsourcing outcomes.

Theoretical framework

Researchers' early work on contingency theory and systems theory grew in significance after the oil crisis of 1973. Kourteli (2000) finds that organisations

are open systems and must interact with their surroundings to survive. This assertion is similar as the main theme of contingency theory. It is widely understood, therefore, that organisations are dependent on their external

environment. Recently, contingency theory has been prevalent in IT studies (Lee et al., 2004). Why is the contingency theory prevalent in the field of IT?
Answering this question, it is necessary to understand the working mechanism
of contingency model. There are many forms of contingency theory. Historically, contingency theory has sought to formulate broad generalizations
about the formal structures that are typically associated with or best fit the use
of different technologies.

There are various outsourcing models in different fields. A contingency outsourcing model used in the IT industry is called the FORT framework (Kishore et al., 2003). Is this FORT framework applicable to the FM sector? The contingency theory is considered to be suitable for various kinds of organisations. The characteristics of the FORT model are based on the contingency approach, according to which there is no single best solution to outsourcing; rather, the best approach is contingent on a number of factors. As discussed, this contingency approach has been widely used in the field of
IT for several years. Finch (2012) claims that firms need to restructure their prediction strategies to survive and to develop. Moreover, this FORT model can initiate to discuss the perspective of outsourcing relationships between the stakeholders in the IT field (Kishore et al., 2003). This can also be applicable to the outsourcing services in the FM industry. Although contingency theory has drawbacks, this principle is considered to be suitable
for more accurate prediction on the future FM outsourcing relationships and
improvement on the quality of future FM outsourcing services. This is the fundamental argument of the study. Hence, a firm's facilities management services must be compatible with the conditions of the market and other external factors. Hitherto this research seeks to map current outsourcing relationships in facilities management, and to predict future FM outsourcing relationships between clients and service providers in the local higher tertiary-
education environment.

Insinga and Werle (2000) argue that one of the key concerns behind outsourcing research is to foster the most appropriate form of relationships between a company and service providers. Hätönen and Eriksson (2009) also
observe that various economic theories are built on the need to explain the management of inter-organizational relations. Theoretical background behind
the different aspects of the outsourcing phenomenon is rather versatile. Accordingly, adopting a singe theoretical view would most probably lead to an
oversimplified analysis, especially given the intention to address the five questions of what, why, where, how and when. Hence, it is imperative to understand five theories from the three stages for the theoretical framework in
this study. Figure 1 indicates the five selected theories for five key outsourcing
questions in this study. This describes a holistic view. Table 1 shows the summary on five theories applying in outsourcing relationships and their functions.

Stage I Stage II Stage III
BIG BANG BAND
WAGON
BARRIERLESS
ORGANIZATIONS ?
RESEARCH
QUESTIONS
WHY?
HOW?
WHAT?
WHERE?
WHEN?
APPLIED THEORIES
Transaction cost Resource View
Organization based Relational
(Agency) view
/ (Social Exchange)
Evolution & learning
(Entrepreneurial)

1950 19
1980 199090 200000 200707
Figure 1 - An overview of the five theories in this study
Theory Definitions Functions
Transaction Cost Economics

Organizational effectiveness depends on choosing the appropriate governance structure (internal vs. external), so as to minimize production costs and transaction costs. The level of transaction costs incurred depends on three key transaction attributes—asset specificity, uncertainty, and frequency (Williamson, 1985). Structuring
of outsourcing contracts

Agency Cost Theory

All contracts involve a principal–agent relationship that is characterized by goal incongruence between the principal and the agent. This results in agency costs, specifically, bonding costs (to achieve incentive alignment), monitoring costs (to reduce information asymmetry), and residual loss (due to risk aversion) (Jensen & Meckling, 1976).

Resource Dependency Theory

Firms are dependent on their external environment for resources. Resources that the firm cannot generate internally must be acquired through external acquisition. Firms must therefore actively manage the environment and their resource flow, to minimize dependence (Pfeffer & Salancik, 1978).

Addressing ease of exit

Entrepreneurial Actions

Entrepreneurship is an organizational capability that drives economic growth. Entrepreneurial actions, as a process of creative destruction, involve proactive efforts to discover and exploit market opportunities for innovation (Schumpeter, 1936).

Continuous relationship management and information feedback
Social Exchange Theory

Interorganizational relationships involve not only legal exchanges between the parties, but also social exchanges based on reciprocity. This requires cooperation and give and take between the parties (Blau, 1964).

Table 1 - Summary on five theories in outsourcing relationships
Facilities management outsourcing services in the higher-education sector
Generally, there are some benefits on application of outsourcing in the higher

education sector (Adegoke and Adegoke, 2013). The growing demand of FM supporting services at the local universities in past years was accompanied by

advising deployment of outsourcing approach (University Grants Committee,

2010). Although FM outsourcing services at such institutions are increasing,

very little local empirical research has been conducted into the proportion of

outsourcing services in such institutions. As for the kinds of diversified outsourcing services at the local institutions, there are high risk waste management, landscaping and horticulture, information technology, capital project, cleaning, campus security, catering, maintenance for the building facilities, minor alteration and addition work of premises.

Given that the share of universities' income from tuition fees paid by students

has increased radically over the last 30 years (Carpentier, 2004), the recruitment of students becomes particularly vital. From a FM perspective, Vidalakis et al. (2013) investigate the extent to which the quality of facilities can influence student decision to join a particular higher education institution

because of students' purchase behaviour as an essential determinant of the university marking positioning strategy. Indeed, higher education institutions

facilities and learning spaces are, not as important as the course itself but, certainly one of the main aspects that students consider when deciding to join

a university (Maringe, 2006; Price et al., 2003). Reynolds and Cain (2006) further discover that a quality built environment is not a sufficient, but necessary condition to recruit and retain students. Given the continuous and

increasing pressure on higher education funding, it is imperative to understand the maintenance and procurement on construction of new or refurbishment of existing facilities (Vidalakis et al., 2013).

There are three main reasons for the need to build on this study of FM outsourcing services, particularly in the local higher-education sector. Firstly,
outsourcing is one of the procurement approaches used to provide building operation support services in facilities management. Although outsourcing services may not be the best means of solving the typical strategic and operational problems encountered by facilities managers, use of this sourcing
strategy in the higher-education sector was scarce but more efficient (Adegoke and Adegoke, 2013). Secondly, very little empirical research has been conducted in this area. Vidalakis et al., (2013) claim that further research
is required to reveal the strategic aspects of FM and defines the role of facilities as part of the organisational strategy and culture on improvement of
value for money. Thirdly, organisations currently need to adopt outsourcing to
take care of built environment in their tertiary institutions because they want to
save money (Ferris and Graddy, 1991). Hong Kong's institutions of higher education are no exception. They too need to balance their budgets, and outsourcing allows them to reduce costs. Universities UK (2009) reports that
expenditure on estates and facilities are the second largest cost item after salaries.

Recently, the senior managements of local universities and tertiary institutions
have been advised to outsource FM support services in the campuses (University Grants Committee, 2010). Table 2 shows the grants on the University Grants Committee (UGC) - funded institutions for the past ten years. This reflects UGC-funded institutions urgently requiring substantial new
and improvement works in the institutions' campuses on recent years. In addition, this also reflects that The Hong Kong Special Area Region Government has a great financial burden on higher education of those UGC-funded institutions. As for the relationship between the quality of educational

facilities and resultant educational achievement, there is a growing body of scientific evidence (Duyar, 2010; Fram, 2010; Tanner, 2009). Therefore, investigation on the effect of facility services on academic achievement is worthwhile.

Financial Year

2003

/04

2004

/05

2005

/06

2006

/07

2007

/08

2008

/09

2009

/10

2010

/11

2011

/12

2012

/13 1

Grants for UGC-

funded

Institutions 2

($m)

14628 12487 12978 12540 12479 12808 12816 14228 16335 18920

Capital Grants 3 6.2% 5.1% 5.9% 4.4% 4.5% 5.2% 11.6% 14.5% 25.3% 17.8%

Total

Government

Expenditure 2

($m)

243213 242235 233071 226863 234815 312412 289025 301360 364037 380615

Total Amount of
Grants as %
of Total
Government
Expenditure 4
6.0% 5.2% 5.6% 5.5% 5.3% 4.1% 4.4% 4.7% 4.5% 5.0%
Total Amount of
Grants as %
of Total
Government
Expenditure
on Education 4
25.5% 22.9% 23.9% 24.1% 23.2% 17.1% 22.0% 23.4% 24.1% 24.3%
Notes:
1. To tie in with the implementation of the new academic structure, UGC-funded institutions have
admitted two cohorts of students under the old and new academic structures in the 2012/13
academic year.
2. The figures on Grants to UGC-funded Institutions and Total Government Expenditure refer to the
financial year of the Government from April to March.
3. The figures on Capital Grants cover both grants for capital works projects and Alterations, Additions,
Repairs and Improvements (AA&I) projects.
4. The figures on Total Government Expenditure and Total Government Expenditure on Education are
extracted from The Budget.
Source: University Grants Committee of Hong Kong
Table 2 - Statistics on Grants for University Grants Committee-funded Institutions as a whole, 2003-04 to 2012-13
Critical issues for successful outsourcing
Following the publication of a number of seminal studies on facilities management in recent decades, researchers have undertaken many
significant explorations of outsourcing. The literature focuses mainly on the reasons for outsourcing, its pros and cons and its critical success factors, and
on determining which activities tend to be outsourced in particular

industries
(Boyson et al., 1999). However, these studies neglect to examine the link between outsourcing arrangements and the performance of service providers.
Coenen et al. (2010) argue that FM corporations should work on managing profitable customer relationships to ensure outsourcing success. Investigation
into FM outsourcing relationship types between client and service provider has been initiated on improving service efficiency in specific business.

Although outsourcing has been discussed from many perspectives in different
fields, some firms continue to be disadvantaged by the unsatisfactory performance of their outsourcing service providers. As more organisations made the transition to outsourced FM services, the number of reported cases
of failure was also increasing (Brown, 2002; Chan, 2008). Baithélemy (2003)
address seven common problems for most failed outsourcing efforts. Plane and Green (2012) also explain that the relationships between clients and contractors did not always prosper as anticipated. Hence, there is still possibly
a hidden problem on outsourcing failure not yet be observed and solved.
Kavčič and Tavčar (2008) claim that outsourcing can increase an organisation's short-term gains especially in financial terms. However, it may
also ruin the company's reputation and success due to poor-quality performance and hidden difficulties. Such problems can exceed the short-term benefits of outsourcing. They also state that trust, based on the mutual long- term interest of both participants, is an important factor determining the
success of the relationship between an outsourcing company and an outsourcer. Poor management of the relationship between outsourcers and stakeholders is one possible reason for outsourcing failures; however, no detailed investigations of this topic have recently been undertaken. Moreover,
Marshall et al. (2004) report that process studies of outsourcing are rare. It is
suggested to use a structured procedure capable of controlling the evolution

of a generic outsourcing process (Kakabadse and Kakabadse, 2000).
However, there is only limited research on structured partnerships in the field
of FM services (Lehtonen and Salonen, 2005). This suggests that our existing
knowledge of best-fit FM outsourcing with regard to service providers, clients
and users is inadequate and under-developed. It is necessary not only to
develop new skills for managing outsourcing relationships, but also to develop
the capability to utilise these skills effectively (Harland et al. 2005). The
relationship between the company and the service provider should be taken
into account when addressing facility-related services (Cigolini et. al.,
2011).
Plane and Green (2012) also claim that benefits of such relationships in the
context of FM procurement, for which partnering and collaboration are
essential.

The performance of service providers can affect the quality of FM services,
which in turn influences client satisfaction. There is a knowledge gap
concerning the link between outsourcing arrangements and service provider
performance or client satisfaction (Cigolini, et al., 2011, Jensen, et al. 2012,
Lehtonen and Salonen, 2005; Plane, and Green, 2012). The objective of this
study is to close this gap. Good relationship management, collaboration and
trust-building activities are shown to be just as important as delivering the
agreed FM services (Jensen et al., 2012; Kadefors, 2008). The drive towards
partnering and collaborative working practices continues to gain pace. For
example, the PAS 11000 standard for collaborative business relationship
management was introduced as a formal British Standard in December 2010
(British Standards Institute, 2010), and is described in an FM World article
as
being 'perfectly logical for the FM sector' (FM World, 2010). Hence,
examination of the relationship between outsourcing modes and the
performance of FM service providers is needed. Lok et al. (2010) suggest that
outsourcing practices can affect outsourcing-relationship types and thus the
profit equations of organisations. Clients openly and regularly review their

relationships with service providers.

CHAPTER FOUR

Critical analysis of the outsourcing models

Outsourcing activities to a service provider can obviously benefit companies in
terms of cost estimation, due to the service provider's familiarity with the work
environment and conditions of the installations (Lai, Yik and Jones, 2008). FM
outsourcing is an example of the professional mode, with service providers' taking the leading role in professional decision making. However, the poor performance of outsourced service providers cannot be eliminated, and this may pose unforeseen challenges. Scholars continue to debate the question of
why so many outsourcing failures are reported if the professional mode constructs the optimal relationship between clients and service providers.

Is it necessary to establish a specific outsourcing-relationship model for facilities management? Before answering this question, it is important to discuss the various possible kinds of outsourcing failures. Baithélemy (2003)
claims that one or more of seven problems are responsible for most failed outsourcing efforts, and that firms are generally reluctant to report outsourcing
failures. Hätönen and Eriksson (2009) observe that the dynamics and management of outsourcing relationships are very important issues to have become a key managerial interest. The management of the relationships with
key suppliers is likely to become increasingly important (Kakabadse and Kakabadse, 2002). The question of how the outsourcing process is carried

out

is connected to the relationship between the outsourcer and the provider. For

example, studying the process in an international context (and thus combining

the questions of how and where outsourcing takes place) may shed new light

on the outsourcing strategy. Harland et al. (2005) claim that the management

of outsourcing relationships, along with the outsourcing process itself, is one

of the essential themes of outsourcing research. However, insufficient

attention has been paid to outsourcing failures from the perspective of outsourcing hidden relationships in the entrepreneurial environment (Ikediashi

et. al., 2012 and 2013). Establishing a specific outsourcing-relationship model

for facilities management may not be the final answer, but it can at least help us to explain and interpret the unseen and complicated scenarios involved.

In short, five outsourcing models are updated in various industries from logistics, different fields, IT, operations management and supply-chain management, but each of which has its own deficiencies. For example, in the

field of logistics, prescriptive models of decision making cannot be accurately

aligned with outsourcing practice. In the field of IT, the outsourcing relationship

management model does not accommodate all of the relationships between vendors and clients at different stages of the framework. The model of four outsourced-outsourcer relationship types does not reflect the evolution of outsourcing relationships.

Consequently, the aim of this research is to apply the most suitable model's

rationale to the FM sector. A framework of four outsourcing relationships types

(FORT) in the IT industry was proposed (Kishore et al., 2003). This FORT model is used to provide insight into the types of outsourcing relationships exist between clients and service providers. The most interesting trait of

this
model is that it examines the evolution of companies' outsourcing
relationships. Outsourcing relationships are not static; they are liable to
change and evolve over time due to changes in the external environment
and
in clients' internal requirements (Kishore et al., 2003). Unlike the FORT
model,
other models are not dynamic in nature and do not explore the development
of companies' outsourcing relationships. This study examines the FORT
model in the specific context of the FM industry. This model is suitable and
original because the proposed model covers the relationships between
outsourcing types and outsourcing practices. Further arguments are
provided
to support the model of four outsourcing-relationship types. Every
outsourcing
model has its own advantages, because of its particular characteristics and
theoretical underpinnings, but also its own disadvantages. Determining
which
model is generally best, therefore, is rather a complicated process. Lok and
Finch (2012) state that the FORT model is particularly applicable to the FM
sector on account of the specific advantages. Table 3 indicates the
advantages and characteristics of the FORT Framework related to
outsourcing relationships in a FM contract.

The FORT Framework
Advantages Characteristics
Like an x-ray machine · Clearly explains and interprets the invisible and
complicated
scenarios
· Identifies each stage between the contractual parties
Efficient differentiation
of contracts
· Interpret several kinds of FM contracts simultaneously
according to the four relationship types
Easy to handle · Simultaneously check the degree of responsibility and
the
strategic effect on the service providers' outsourced portfolio
Effective · Check and update the outsourcing relationships between
clients and service providers for each specific FM contract

Versatile · Conveniently applied in different industries
User-friendly · Easy to understand and apply
Flexible · No time constraints on contracts required
Most reliable · Oldest of the five models identified
· Commonly applied in the IT industry
Table 3 - Advantages and characteristics of the FORT Framework

CHAPTER FIVE

The FORT model in facilities management

In the context of the IT industry, the FORT framework is contingent in nature.
Finch (2012) explains that outsourcing relationships have increasingly come
to entail processes of mutual support and nurturing. This may include the
enhancement of customer relations, improved supplier relationships and the
improvement of product or service offerings. Figure 2 indicates the FORT
Framework applicable to the FM industry. This new tailor-made proposed FM
framework is called Contingency Outsourcing Relationship (CORE) model.
Ownership and /or control of various FM

High
Outsource requiring service
provider's more commitment
(Reliance)
    Partner having common goals
(Alliance)
    assets
transferred
to service
providers
Low
    In-house
(Support)

Outsource enabling acquiring
service provider's technical
expertise
(Alignment)
Low High
Influence of the outsourced FM portfolio on the firm's
competitive positioning and its long-term strategy
Remarks:
(IT dimension): e.g. (Support)
FM dimension: e.g. In-house
Figure 2 - The FORT Framework suitable for FM industry (The CORE model)
Kishore et al. (2003) explain the mechanism of the FORT model. In the case of support and alignment relationships, clients make little investment in service provider specific assets when the level of service-provider involvement
is low. In such cases, client-provider relationships usually operate in the short
term and are fairly specific to outsourced projects and services. Hence, there
is little need for incentives and penalties to be specified in detail. However, when the level of service-provider involvement is high, clients make large investments in service provider specific assets. For example, clients become more committed to financing service providers' equipment, technology, systems and skills as part of reliance and alliance connections, which leads to
a locked-in relationship. Williamson (1981) describes this phenomenon as 'small numbers opportunism'. Within the alliance relationship, trust is an important mechanism for ensuring that service providers' interests coincide
with clients' interests (Sabherwal, 1999).

CHAPTER SIX

Research strategy

In researching the field of management, a researcher needs to adopt many strategies. Yin (2003) claims that a research strategy should be chosen as a function of the research situation. This section is to discuss the justification of

selection on appropriate strategies in this study. The relevant key points are listed as the followings.

l Importance on selection of suitable research strategy

There are different ways of collecting and analyzing empirical evidence of the research interest. Research strategy is a way of going about one's research, embodying a particular style and employing different research methods (Remenyi et al., 1998). In order to achieve the study aim and objectives, it is imperative to set optimum research strategy. However, there are a number of criteria needed in consideration such as scope and nature of data required for a particular methodology, resource constraints in terms of time and finance and researcher's personal experience, knowledge and skills (Remenyi et al., 1998; Yin, 2003). In summary, the scope and nature of data of this study are based at the opinions from the service providers and clients. The research study period is very tight and research budget is very limited.

l Various types of research strategy

There are many strategies including experiment, case study, survey, and ethnography (Remenyi et al., 1998; Saunders et al., 2003; Yin, 2003). Each strategy has its own specific approach to collect and to analyse empirical data, and each one has its own specific advantages and disadvantages. However, most of these strategies are not suitably applied for the aim and objectives of this research.

i) As for experiments, two main features are manipulation and control but it is inappropriate to set up a laboratory to collect the data in this study. The reason is that experiments fall under the positivist research approach normally used in natural science studies and typically involve two or more experimental groups and a control group. One drawback of experiments is that a laboratory setting is often different from the real world (Collis and Hussey, 2003). The nature of this study is about business management but not natural science.

ii) As for case study, the researcher has `no control over events' and the

questions relating to 'why', 'what', or 'how' deal with operational links needing to be traced over time (Yin, 2003). Again, this approach is inappropriate to conduct data collection in this study because the researcher can only focus on a contemporary phenomenon within a real-life context in frequency. In business studies, a common case is a company or parts of a company, but it can also be other things, such as a group of people or event. Some drawbacks of using this strategy include difficulties in finding organisations that are willing to participate in the study; it is difficult to understand the events in a particular period of time. The fact is that it is difficult to identify the suitable local organizations participating in the research as a case study. Moreover, the shortcoming of case studies is described as very time consuming and costly (Collis and Hussey, 2003; Saunders et al., 2003).

iii) Generally speaking, survey is one of the positivist approaches to research. Although this approach has some weaknesses such as low response rate and possible ambiguities in the questions, the benefits such as low cost, convenient access to respondents, mass production, high consistency of research questions, no limitation on time of delivery of questionnaires and completion of questionnaires and fast dispatching of a survey strategy suggested that it was the appropriate methodology in this case. Indeed, surveys are the most popular and commonly used method in business and management research (Remenyi et al., 1998; Saunders et al., 2003).

In this study, the selected number of service providers and staffs in FM department of clients from the local tertiary institutes and universities in the

questionnaire surveys are the sample to be taken as a representative of the whole population.

CHAPTER SEVEN

Methodological approach

This study tests whether the Four Outsourcing Relationship Types (FORT) model is applicable to the FM services of Hong Kong's higher education sector through characterising the FM outsourcing relationship types. Ikediashi
et al. (2013) consider the importance of outsourcing risks for achieving outsourcing success in the FM sector. In order to holistically build a model for
outsourcing FM services, FM strategists should also understand the outsourcing success variables. This study can, in the other way, contribute to
existing research on FM by developing another hypothesized model to investigate the hidden relationships between outsourcing success variables and their impact on firm performance in terms of time and strategy. In the following sections, there is an analysis of outsourcing relationship from these
theoretical perspectives to develop corollaries about the relationships between
the strategic manoeuvres identified and the different dimensions of outsourcing relationship. There are nine corollaries in this research. Table 4 summarizes the theories discussed, the key concepts used, and the resulting corollaries developed.

Theory /
Concept
Key concepts / Strategic
Manoeuvres
Corollaries
Four FM
outsourcing

dimensions

FM strategists and types of FM
outsourcing contract → FM
outsourcing dimensions

(Clients and Service providers) C1a, C1b: Clients' and Service providers' evaluations regarding four
outsourcing relationship dimensions rendered to them are not different according to the background of
construction professionals and types of current outsourcing contracts.

Transaction Cost
Economics

Reduced asset specificity by
minimizing customization →
outsourcing relationship

(Clients and Service providers) C2a, C2b: Clients' and Service providers' evaluations regarding
minimizing customization rendered to them are not different according to the background of construction
professionals and types of current outsourcing contracts.

Agency Cost Theory

Reduced monitoring cost by
enhancing process maturity →
outsourcing relationship
Mitigation of residual loss by retaining
in-house competence → outsourcing
relationship

(Clients & Service providers) C3a, C3b: Clients' and Service providers' evaluations regarding enhancing
process maturity rendered to them are not different according to the background of construction
professionals and types of current outsourcing contracts.
(Clients and Service providers) C4a, C4b: Clients' and Service providers' evaluations regarding retaining
in-house competence rendered to them are not different according to the background of construction
professionals and types of current outsourcing contracts.

Resource Dependency Theory

Diluting supplier concentration
through multiple sourcing →
outsourcing relationship
Reduced switching costs through
vendor interoperability
→ outsourcing relationship
(Clients and Service providers) C5a, C5b: Clients' and Service providers'
evaluations regarding multiple
sourcing rendered to them are not different according to the background of
construction professionals
and types of current outsourcing contracts.
(Clients and Service providers) C6a, C6b: Clients' and Service providers'
evaluations regarding
leveraging on vendor interoperability rendered to them are not different
according to the background of
construction professionals and types of current outsourcing contracts.
Entrepreneurial
Actions
Enhanced entrepreneurial capability
through proactive sensing →
outsourcing relationship
(Clients and Service providers) C7a, C7b: Clients' and Service providers'
evaluations regarding proactive
sensing rendered to them are not different according to the background of
construction professionals and
types of current outsourcing contracts.
Social Exchange
Theory
Building relational reciprocity
through enhanced partnership
quality → outsourcing relationship
(Clients and Service providers) C8a, C8b: Clients' and Service providers'
evaluations regarding
enhancing partnership quality rendered to them are not different according
to the background of
construction professionals and types of current outsourcing contracts.
The FORT
model

Outsourcing relationship dimensions
→ outsourcing relationship types
(Clients and Service providers) C9: Outsourcing relationship dimensions (Ownership, Control,
Competitive Position and Long Term Plan) is related to outsourcing relationship types and the strength of
the relationships is moderated by those outsourcing types.

Table 4 - Summary of corollaries on outsourcing relationship

Strategic manoeuvres for outsourcing relationship: a conceptual framework
There are two parts composing the research model in this study. This first part
is about outsourcing relationships and the second part is about outsourcing category. With the combination of two parts, a research model was developed
for this study. It firstly sets out the relationships between the independent variable (outsourcing relationship manoeuvres) and dependent variable (four
outsourcing relationship dimensions). It secondly sets out the relationships between the independent variable (four outsourcing relationship dimensions)
and dependent variable (outsourcing category). The interaction and combined
effect of these independent variables will determine the value of the
dependent variables for the two parts.

In the first part of the model, the factors perceived to be of principal relevance
were discussed. Outsourcing relationships include two parts: extent of substitution and strategic importance or impact. The four relationship dimensions can be measured objectively and subjectively and they are inter-related and intra-related. These factors can form the dependent variables of this part. Outsourcing relationship manoeuvres are supported by five identified
theories. These factors form the independent variables of this part. In the second part of the model, the factors perceived to be of principal relevance were discussed. Outsourcing category of a project includes in-house, service provider with commitment, service provider with technical expertise and partner. The factors can be measured objectively and subjectively and they

are inter-related and intra-related. These factors can form the dependent variables of this part. Again, outsourcing relationships include two parts: extent of substitution and strategic importance or impact. The four relationship
dimensions can be measured objectively and subjectively and they are inter-related and intra-related. These factors form the independent variables of this
part. Figure 3 provides a graphic representation of the strategic manoeuvres and the theoretical perspectives from which they are derived.

Corollary 1 (Relationships between four outsourcing relationships measured by critical success
factors for outsourcing strategies and two FM stakeholders)
Corollary 2 – Corollary 8 (Relationships between five outsourcing manoeuvres and two FM
stakeholders)
Corollary 9 (Relationships between four outsourcing relationships measured by critical success
factors for outsourcing strategies and four FM outsourcing categories)
C9 C7 C8 C5 & C6
Four Outsourcing
Relationship Dimensions
Extent of substitution: Ownership & Control
Strategic impact: Competitive position &
Long term plan
Outsourcing Categories
Inhouse (Support), SP with technical expertise
(Alignment), SP with commitment (Reliance) &
Partner (Alliance)
Transaction
Cost
Economics
Minimizing
customization
(asset
specificity)
Enhancing process
maturity
(information asymmetry)

Retaining in-house
competence
(residual loss)
Proactive sensing
(entrepreneurial capability)
Enhanced partnership
quality
Social Exchange Theory Entrepreneurial Actions
Agency Cost Theory
C2
C3 & 4
Background
C1

Figure 3: Research model on contingency model for outsourcing relationships in FM sector

CHAPTER EIGHT

Testing the nine proposed corollaries

The main objective of this section is to test the nine corollaries concerning the
determinants of outsourcing relationship dimensions, strategic manoeuvres,
clients' and service providers' evaluation regarding outsourcing category and
outsourcing relationship types. The statistical techniques employed for testing
these corollaries 1 to 8 are the Mann-Whitney U test (only two groups of
continuous variables in the background of construction professionals) and
Kruskal-Wallis test (continuous variable for three or more groups in the types
of current outsourcing contracts) and corollary 9 is Multi-nominal Logistic
Regression (similar to logistic regression, but more general as the dependent
variable not restricted to two categories in four outsourcing categories). Nine
main corollaries have been tested as follows.

Testing the corollary 1

As seen earlier, researchers and practitioners have found that IT clients
consider four dimensions in their assessments of outsourcing category
between clients and service providers (Kishore et. al., 2003).

* Support: requiring assistance
* Alignment: technical expertise
* Reliance: service commitment
* Alliance: common goals

Client and Service Provider - C1 (a)

The Mann-Whitney test has been used to test for differences between two independent groups on a continuous measure. There is no statistical significant difference with a two-tailed p value. The probability value (p) is not

less than or equal to 0.05, that to say there is no statistically significant difference in the perceived four outsourcing relationship dimensions rendered

to two kinds of FM strategists.

Performance of

Outsourcing Services

Evaluation of outsourcing categories on

current & future FM contracts of clients and

service providers

Characteristics of

FM strategists in

clients & Service

Providers (SP)

Resource Dependency

Theory

Multiple sourcing

(supplier concentration)

Leveraging vendor

interoperability

(switching costs)

Result on Nonparametric Tests (Clients and Service providers - C1a): Mann-

Whitney U Test comparing four FM outsourcing relationship dimensions in FM

professions of building and building services

Client and Service Provider - C1 (b)

To test the validity of this hypothesis, the Kruskal-Wallis test was used to examine the differences of FM strategists' evaluation of the four outsourcing

relationship dimensions rendered to them in different types of current outsourcing contracts. There is no statistical significant difference with a p value. The probability value (p) is not less than or equal to 0.05. There are no

significant statistical differences in FM strategists' evaluation of the four outsourcing relationship dimensions rendered to them in different types of current outsourcing contracts. This means that all types of profession render

the same perceived four outsourcing relationship dimensions from the FM strategists' point of view, in terms of the outsourcing contracts.

Result on Nonparametric Tests (Clients and Service providers - C1b): Kruskal-

Wallis Test comparing four FM outsourcing relationship dimensions in four FM

Outsourcing contracts (Building maintenance, Security, Cleaning and Catering)

Testing corollaries 2 to 8

Clients and Service Providers (C2a – C8a)

The Mann-Whitney test has been used to test for differences of the perceived

strategic manoeuvres (Five theories) rendered to two kinds of FM strategists.

Result on Nonparametric Tests (Clients and Service providers): Mann-Whitney

U Test comparing strategic manoeuvres (Five theories) in FM professions of

building and building services

Clients and Service Providers (C2b – C8b)

To test the validity of this hypothesis, the Kruskal-Wallis test was used to examine the differences of FM strategists' evaluation of the strategic

manoeuvres (Five theories) rendered to them in different types of current outsourcing contracts.

Result on Nonparametric Tests (Clients and Service providers): Kruskal-Wallis

Test comparing strategic manoeuvres (Five theories) in four FM Outsourcing

contracts (Building maintenance, Security, Cleaning and Catering)

Testing corollary 9

Dependent variable: A categorical variable that record whether the strategist

was satisfactory. The value of mulit-Nominal logistic regression may be high (Likert Scale 4 or 5) or low (Likert Scale 1 or 2). For example, the value "1" indicates the high degree of satisfaction of the specific outsourcing category,
while the value "0" indicates the low degree of satisfaction of the specific outsourcing category on contingent approaches of the specific FM outsourcing
contract. In this research, the multi-nominal logistic regression is used to analyse the categories of FM outsourcing relationship types from clients and service providers. This test is used to observe and predict the relationships. Table 5 shows the data analysis of Multi-Nominal Logistic Regression.

Types of
Variable
Variables
(Client)
Variables
(Service
Provider)
Definition
Factors Y1 – Y4 Y1 – Y4 Types of FM Contract
Y1: Building maintenance
Y2: Security
Y3: Cleaning
Y4: Catering
Dependent OC1 – OC4 OC1 – OC4 FM Outsourcing Categories
In-house team, Commitment,
Technical expertise, Common goals
Independent SO1 – SO5 SO1 – SO5
FM Outsourcing Dimensions
Ownership of FM assets
Independent SC1 – SC8 SC1 – SC3 Control of FM assets
Independent CP1 – CP6 CP1 – CP17 Influence on competitive position
Independent LP1 – LP8 LP1 – LP11 Influence on long term plan
Table 5 - Factors, dependent variables and independent variables in Multi-Nominal Logistic Regression

Category of outsourcing relationship of a specific kind of outsourcing contract

between client and service provider
Client
To predict the category of the outsourcing relationships, the Mulit-Nominal
Logistic Regression was used to determine the different types of current
crucial outsourcing contracts between the clients and service providers
from
the perspective of clients. The types of outsourcing category on clients'
point
of views will be investigated by applying the FM outsourcing relationship
dimensions in four FM outsourcing contracts through mulit-Nominal
Logistic
Regression. Table 6 indicates the details of data from this Regression. There
are total 188 valid cases and 14 missing cases from the clients' respondents.
According to the case processing summary, the model category is Technical
Expertise, with 33.5% of the cases. Thus, the null model classifies correctly
33.5% of the time. This classification table shows the practical results of
using
the multinomial logistic regression model.
    Number
of case
    Marginal
Percentage
Types of outsourcing category Inhouse 46 24.5%
Service commitment 41 21.8%
Technical expertise 63 33.5%
Common goals 38 20.2%
    Measurement of Ownership of
various FM assets transferred by you
    low 80 42.6%
high 108 57.4%
    Measurement of Control of various
FM assets transferred by you
    low 56 29.8%
high 132 70.2%
    Measurement of influence of the
outsourced FM portfolio on our
competitive position

low 75 39.9%
high 113 60.1%
Measurement of influence of the
outsourced FM portfolio on our long-
term plan
low 62 33.0%
high 126 67.0%
Valid 188 100.0%
Missing 14
Total 202
Subpopulation 25 a
a. The dependent variable has only one value observed in 2 (8.0%) subpopulations.
Table 6 - Case Processing Summary (Clients)
Table 7 indicates the observed and predicted frequencies on category of FM

outsourcing relationship types from clients. On prediction of the type of future
building maintenance, security, cleaning and catering contracts, there is an inclination to the types of inhouse and technical expertise. In summary, degree of importance on the types of inhouse and technical expertise outsourcing categories is the highest to the four FM outsourcing contracts.
(a) (b) (c) (d) (e) Types of outsourcing
category
Frequency Percentage
(f) (g) Pearson
Residual
(f) (g)
Building
maintenance
low low low low Inhouse 3 3.100 -.065 21.4% 22.1%
low low high high Service commitment 0 .035 -.189 .0% 1.8%
high high high low Technical expertise 1 .908 .110 25.0% 22.7%
high high high high Common goals 6 5.374 .291 15.8% 14.1%
Security low low low low Inhouse 3 3.082 -.053 21.4% 22.0%
low low high high Service commitment 0 .030 -.175 .0% 1.5%
high high high low Technical expertise 1 .977 .027 25.0% 24.4%

high high high high Common goals 3 3.979 -.531 11.1% 14.7%

Cleaning low low low low Inhouse 3 2.401 .437 27.3% 21.8%

low low high high Service commitment 0 .026 -.163 .0% 1.3%

high high high low Technical expertise 1 1.567 -.527 16.7% 26.1%

high high high high Common goals 3 3.668 -.379 12.5% 15.3%

Catering low low low low Inhouse 2 1.295 .699 33.3% 21.6%

low low high high Service commitment 0 .022 -.151 .0% 1.1%

high high high low Technical expertise 2 2.224 -.177 25.0% 27.8%

high high high high Common goals 0 .158 -.433 .0% 15.8%

The percentages are based on total observed frequencies in each subpopulation.

Remarks: a) Major types of FM outsourcing contract in the questionnaire survey; b) Influence

of the outsourced FM portfolio on our long-term plan; c) Influence of the outsourced FM

portfolio on our competitive position; d) Control of various FM assets transferred by you; e)

Ownership of various FM assets transferred by you; f) Observed and g) Predicted

Table 7 - Observed and Predicted Frequencies on category of FM outsourcing relationship types from clients

Service Provider

To predict the category of the outsourcing relationships, the Mulit-Nominal Logistic Regression was used to determine the different types of current crucial outsourcing contracts between the clients and service providers from

the perspective of service provider. The types of outsourcing category on service provider's point of views will be investigated by applying the FM outsourcing relationship dimensions in four FM outsourcing contracts through

mulit-Nominal Logistic Regression. Table 8 indicates the details of data from

this Regression. There are total 160 valid cases and 3 missing cases from the service providers' respondents. According to the case processing summary, the model category is Inhouse, with 29.4% of the cases. Thus, the null model

classifies correctly 29.4% of the time. This classification table shows the practical results of using the multinomial logistic regression model.

Number
of case
    Marginal
Percentage
Types of outsourcing category Inhouse 47 29.4%
Service commitment 41 25.6%
Technical expertise 40 25.0%
Common goals 32 20.0%
    Measurement of Ownership of
various FM assets transferred by you
    low 10 6.3%
high 150 93.8%
    Measurement of Control of various
FM assets transferred by you
    low 16 10.0%
high 144 90.0%
    Measurement of Influence of the
outsourced FM portfolio on our
competitive position
    low 10 6.3%
high 150 93.8%
    Measurement of Influence of the
outsourced FM portfolio on our long-
term plan
    low 10 6.3%
high 150 93.8%
Valid 160 100.0%
Missing 3
Total 163
Subpopulation 10 a
    a. The dependent variable has only one value observed in 1 (10.0%)
subpopulations.
Table 8 - Case Processing Summary (Service provider)
    If the significance value is small (less than 0.05), then the model does
not
adequately fit the data. In this case, table 9 indicates its value greater than
0.1, so the data are consistent with the model assumptions. The Pearson
residual is a measure of the difference between the observed and predicted

values. Large Pearson residuals can indicate covariate patterns that are not well fit by the model. In classification and validation, cross tabulating observed

response categories with predicted categories helps to determine how well the

model identifies clients' and service providers' preferences.

Chi-Square df Sig.

Clients Pearson 17.803 57 1.000

Deviance 19.588 57 1.000

Service

providers

Pearson 3.902 18 1.000

Deviance 4.659 18 .999

Table 9 - Goodness-of-Fit (Clients and Service providers)

Table 10 indicates the observed and predicted frequencies on category of FM

outsourcing relationship types from service providers. On prediction of the future building maintenance, security, cleaning and catering contracts, there is

an equally inclination to the type of inhouse outsourcing category. In summary,

degree of importance on the types of inhouse and common goals outsourcing

categories is the highest to the four FM outsourcing contracts.

(a) (b) (c) (d) (e) Types of

outsourcing

category

Frequency Percentage

(f) (g) Pearson

Residual

(f) (g)

Building

maintenance

low low low low Inhouse 2 1.999 .001 50.0% 50.0%

high high high high Common goals 12 11.066 .311 20.0% 18.4%

Security low low low low Inhouse 1 1.000 .000 50.0% 50.0%

high high high low Technical

expertise

1 .833 .200 20.0% 16.7%
high high high high Common goals 6 6.552 -.239 17.1% 18.7%
Cleaning low low low low Inhouse 1 1.000 -.001 50.0% 50.0%
high high high high Common goals 4 4.370 -.197 17.4% 19.0%
Catering low low low low Inhouse 1 1.001 -.001 50.0% 50.0%
high high high high Common goals 5 5.012 -.006 19.2% 19.3%

The percentages are based on total observed frequencies in each subpopulation.

Remarks: a) Major types of FM outsourcing contract in the questionnaire survey;b) Influence

of the outsourced FM portfolio on our long-term plan; c) Influence of the outsourced FM

portfolio on our competitive position;d) Control of various FM assets transferred by you; e)

Ownership of various FM assets transferred by you; f) Observed and g) Predicted

Table 10 - Observed and Predicted Frequencies on category of FM outsourcing relationship types from service providers

CHAPTER NINE

Findings

The local Government funded vocational training institutes and seven universities in this study represent more than 90% of the FM industry in Hong
Kong's higher educational sectors. The total number in the study sample was
38 FM respondents from clients and 34 FM respondents from service providers who participated in this study. The main outputs of frequency analysis reveal that the study sample was biased towards the master degree holders, where the percentage of those FM professionals (clients and service
providers) was very high being 74% and 64% respectively, and the study sample was well educated. With regard to the FM working experience of the respondents, it has been indicated that almost 60% of the clients' respondents
had equal or more than three years; the percentage of service providers' respondents who had equal or more than three years was 80%.

Results of testing corollaries 1 – 8 (clients)
Table 11 summarises the results of analysis on the types of outsourcing category on the FM relationship from clients. According to the evaluations of
clients' construction professionals on the ownership of various FM assets transferred, infrastructure technology, computing system and communication
system rendered to them are same, but professional knowledge and efficiency
of equipment rendered to them are different. As for the types of current outsourcing contracts on the same dimension, professional knowledge, infrastructure technology, computing system, communication system and

efficiency of equipment rendered to the clients are same.

Corollaries (1 – 8) Results

Ownership of various FM assets transferred

C1a: Clients' evaluations regarding ownership (professional knowledge and efficiency of equipment) rendered to them are not different according to the background of construction professionals.

Rejected

C1a: Clients' evaluations regarding ownership (infrastructure technology,

computing system and communication system) rendered to them are not different according to the background of construction professionals.

Accepted

C1b: Clients' evaluations regarding ownership (professional knowledge, infrastructure technology, computing system, communication system and efficiency of equipment) rendered to them are not different according to the types of current outsourcing contracts.

Accepted

Control of various FM assets transferred

C1a: Clients' evaluations regarding control (infrastructure and equipment) rendered to them are not different according to the background of construction professionals.

Rejected

C1a: Clients' evaluations regarding control (human resources, daily routine operation, job, deadlines, co-ordination meetings and expense) rendered to them are not different according to the background of construction professionals.

Accepted

C1b: Clients' evaluations regarding control (infrastructure, equipment, human resources, daily routine operation, job, deadlines, co-ordination meetings and expense) rendered to them are not different according to the types of current outsourcing contracts.

Accepted

Influence of the outsourced FM portfolio on competitive position

C1a and C1b: Clients' evaluations regarding competitive position (competence, accuracy, productivity, technical competence, comprehensive service and time frame) rendered to them are not different according to the background of construction professionals and types of current outsourcing contracts.

Accepted

Influence of the outsourced FM portfolio on our long-term plan
C1a: Clients' evaluations regarding long-term plan (policy and plan)
Rejected

rendered to them are not different according to the background of construction professionals.

C1a: Clients' evaluations regarding long-term plan (work, safety and health, human resources, administration, quality and environmental protection) rendered to them are not different according to the background of construction professionals.

Accepted

C1b: Clients' evaluations regarding long-term plan (policy, plan, work, safety and health, human resources, administration, quality and environmental protection) rendered to them are not different according to the types of current outsourcing contracts.

Accepted

C2a and C2b: Clients' evaluations regarding minimizing process customization rendered to them are not different according to the background of construction professionals and types of current outsourcing contracts.

Accepted

C3a and C3b: Clients' evaluations regarding enhancing process maturity rendered to them are not different according to the background of construction professionals and types of current outsourcing contracts.

Accepted

C4a and C4b: Clients' evaluations regarding retaining in-house competence rendered to them are not different according to the background of construction professionals and types of current outsourcing contracts.

Accepted

C5a and C5b: Clients' evaluations regarding multiple sourcing rendered to them are not different according to the background of construction professionals and types of current outsourcing contracts.

Accepted

C6a and C6b: Clients' evaluations regarding leveraging on vendor interoperability rendered to them are not different according to the background of construction professionals and types of current outsourcing contracts.

Accepted

C7a and C7b: Clients' evaluations regarding proactive sensing rendered to them are not different according to the background of construction professionals and types of current outsourcing contracts.

Accepted

C8a and C8b: Clients' evaluations regarding enhancing partnership quality rendered to them are not different according to the background of construction professionals and types of current outsourcing contracts.

Accepted

Table 11 - Analysis on the types of outsourcing category on the FM relationship by clients

According to the evaluations of clients' construction professionals on the control of various FM assets transferred, human resources, daily routine operation, job, deadlines, co-ordination meetings and expense are same, but infrastructure and equipment rendered to them are different. As for the types

of current outsourcing contracts on the same dimension, infrastructure, equipment, human resources, daily routine operation, job, deadlines, co-ordination meetings and expense rendered to the clients are same.

According to the evaluations of clients' construction professionals and types of

current outsourcing contracts on the influence of the outsourced FM portfolio

on competitive position, competence, accuracy, productivity, technical competence, comprehensive service and time frame rendered to the clients are same.

According to the evaluations of clients' construction professionals on the influence of the outsourced FM portfolio on our long-term plan, policy and plan

rendered to them are different. As for the evaluations of clients' construction

professionals and types of current outsourcing contracts on the same dimension, policy, plan, work, safety and health, human resources, administration, quality and environmental protection, minimizing process customization, enhancing process maturity, retaining in-house competence, multiple sourcing, leveraging on vendor interoperability, proactive sensing, enhancing partnership quality rendered to the clients are same.

Results of testing corollaries 1 – 8 (service providers)
Table 12 summarises the results of analysis on the types of outsourcing category on the FM relationship from service providers. According to the evaluations of service providers' construction professionals and the types of
current outsourcing contracts on the ownership of various FM assets transferred, equipment or machinery, professional knowledge, completion on
request, capability, resources, rendered to them are same.
Corollaries (1 – 8) Results
Ownership of various FM assets transferred
C1a and C1b: Service providers' evaluations regarding ownership (equipment or machinery, professional knowledge, completion on request, capability and resources) rendered to them are not different according to the background of construction professionals and types of current outsourcing contracts.
Accepted
Control of various FM assets transferred
C1a and C1b: Service providers' evaluations regarding control (professional knowledge, finishing on time and co-ordination meetings) rendered to them are not different according to the background of construction professionals and types of current outsourcing contracts.
Accepted
Influence of the outsourced FM portfolio on competitive position
C1a and C1b: Service providers' evaluations regarding competitive position (financial capability, human resources, assistance, capability, accuracy, productivity, technical competence, focus, responsibility, conduct, courteousness, understanding, comprehensive service, responsibilities, quality, satisfaction and expectation) rendered to them are
Accepted

not different according to the background of construction professionals and types of current outsourcing contracts.
Influence of the outsourced FM portfolio on our long-term plan
C1a and C1b: Service providers' evaluations regarding long-term plan (competing job, policy, plan, work, safety and health, human resources, administration, quality, social responsibility, value-added services and environmental protection) rendered to them are not different according to

the background of construction professionals and types of current outsourcing contracts.

Accepted

C2a and C2b: Service providers' evaluations regarding minimizing process
customization rendered to them are not different according to the
background of construction professionals and types of current outsourcing
contracts.

Accepted

C3a and C3b: Service providers' evaluations regarding enhancing process
maturity rendered to them are not different according to the background of
construction professionals and types of current outsourcing contracts.

Accepted

C4a and C4b: Service providers' evaluations regarding retaining in-house
competence rendered to them are not different according to the
background of construction professionals and types of current outsourcing
contracts.

Accepted

C5a and C5b: Service providers' evaluations regarding multiple sourcing
rendered to them are not different according to the background of
construction professionals and types of current outsourcing contracts.

Accepted

C6a and C6b: Service providers' evaluations regarding leveraging on
vendor interoperability rendered to them are not different according to the
background of construction professionals and types of current outsourcing
contracts.

Accepted

C7a and C7b: Service providers' evaluations regarding proactive sensing
rendered to them are not different according to the background of
construction professionals and types of current outsourcing contracts.

Accepted

C8a and C8b: Service providers' evaluations regarding enhancing
partnership quality rendered to them are not different according to the
background of construction professionals and types of current outsourcing
contracts.

Accepted

Table 12 - Analysis on the types of outsourcing category on the FM relationship by service providers
According to the evaluations of service providers' construction professionals
and the types of current outsourcing contracts on the control of various FM assets transferred, professional knowledge, finishing on time and co-ordination meetings rendered to them are same. According to the evaluations
of service providers' construction professionals and the types of current outsourcing contracts on the influence of the outsourced FM portfolio on competitive position, financial capability, human resources, assistance, capability, accuracy, productivity, technical competence, focus, responsibility,
conduct, courteousness, understanding, comprehensive service, responsibilities, quality, satisfaction and expectation rendered to them are same.

According to the evaluations of service providers' construction professionals
and the types of current outsourcing contracts on the influence of the outsourced FM portfolio on our long-term plan, competing job, policy, plan, work, safety and health, human resources, administration, quality, social responsibility, value-added services, environmental protection, minimizing process customization, enhancing process maturity, retaining in-house competence, multiple sourcing, leveraging on vendor interoperability, proactive sensing and enhancing partnership quality rendered to them are same.

Analysis on matching the results of clients and service providers, Corollary 9
A key to analysis is to identify which types of outsourcing relationships have impact on the standard and quality of the outsourcing services in the major FM outsourcing contracts such as building maintenance, security, cleaning and catering in the Hong Kong's higher education industry. From the result, the clients can obtain an understanding of their predicted percentage of the FM outsourcing relationship type for the specific type of FM contract. The service provider can also evaluate the 'future' possible performance in the
specific outsourcing contract.

The Pearson residual is a measure of the difference between the
observed
and predicted values. Small Pearson residuals can indicate covariate
patterns
that are well fit by the model. The types of outsourcing category for the
specific types of FM contract are based by two variables which are the
optimum predicted percentage and the small Pearson residuals. Table 13
indicates the outsourcing relationship type with the predicted highest
degree
of importance of the specific critical FM outsourcing contract from clients
and
service providers. Predicted good FM outsourcing performance on the
specific
outsourcing contract is achieved by matching the predicted type of
outsourcing category from client and relevant service provider. In
summary,
degree of importance on the type of inhouse outsourcing category is the
highest to the future building maintenance, security, cleaning and catering
contracts. On further prediction of these four FM outsourcing contracts,
there
is also an inclination to the type of technical expertise outsourcing category
from clients but to the type of common goals outsourcing category from
service provider.

(a) (b) (c) (d) (e) Types of
outsourcing
category
Clients
Percentage
Service
Provider
Percentage
(f) (g) (f) (g)
Building
maintenance
Low low low low Inhouse 21.4% 22.1% 50.0% 50.0%
High high high low Technical
expertise 25.0% 22.7% - -
high high high high Common goals - - 20.0% 18.4%

Security
low low low low Inhouse 21.4% 22.0% 50.0% 50.0%
high high high low Technical
expertise 25.0% 24.4% - -
high high high high Common goals - - 17.1% 18.7%
Cleaning
low low low low Inhouse 27.3% 21.8% 50.0% 50.0%
high high high low Technical
expertise 16.7% 26.1% - -
high high high high Common goals - - 17.4% 19.0%
Catering
low low low low Inhouse 33.3% 21.6% 50.0% 50.0%
high high high low Technical
expertise 25.0% 27.8% - -
high high high high Common goals - - 19.2% 19.3%
Remarks: a) Major types of FM outsourcing contract in the questionnaire survey; b) Influence
of the outsourced FM portfolio on long-term plan; c) Influence of the outsourced FM portfolio
on competitive position; d) Control of various FM assets transferred; e) Ownership of various
FM assets transferred; f) Observed and g) Predicted
Table 13 - Predicted FM outsourcing relationship types of the FM outsourcing contracts survey in the current Hong Kong's higher education sector

Chapter 10 - Discussion and Conclusion
Understanding on FM outsourcing relationships in Higher Education Sector
The analysis of the simultaneous relationships between FM outsourcing relationship types and dimensions (substitution of ownership, substitution of
control, competitive position and long-term planning) enhances the overall understanding of FM outsourcing relationships. The empirical investigation reveals a significant relationship between FM outsourcing relationship types
and services in the context of Hong Kong's higher education sector. Clients and service providers have indicated that applying the FM outsourcing

relationship types improves the quality of the services. Meanwhile, the results

of the hypotheses testing indicate that FM outsourcing relationship types are

used in related services; that is, the outsourcing categories of a specific FM outsourcing contract will be achieved through prediction at the level of substitution of ownership, substitution of control, competitive positions and

long-term planning.

Importantly, this research establishes a link between 'high quality FM outsourcing service' and potential increases in substitution of ownership, substitution of control, competitive positions and long-term planning. The relationship between FM outsourcing relationship types and service is statistically significant. The majority of previous FM outsourcing studies has

discussed the causes of service providers' substandard outsourcing performance without considering the relationships among the four FM outsourcing relationship dimensions in FM outsourcing contracts. This research investigates these relationships from both the clients and the service

providers' perspectives, with regard to FM outsourcing relationship categories and services.

Chapter 11 - Future research directions

Although the focus of this study is the importance of FM outsourcing relationship types and dimensions in Hong Kong's higher education sector, and their centrality has been confirmed, the researcher believes that the demand and supply of FM services will play a major role in the future of the higher education industry. As previously noted, universities' financial costs have recently increased, which means that the FM client-strategists must plan

updated FM strategies to solve the current and future financial problems. As a

result, further research is required to explore the relationships among critical

FM outsourcing contracts.

Finally, it is not possible for any single study to cover every aspect of a topic,

and this study is no exception. The 'evolution and revolution' of FM
outsourcing relationship types and dimensions will continue, and thus the
35
topic deserves further investigation. For instance, it is important to
investigate
how clients and service providers can manage the financial aspects of FM
outsourcing contracts to efficiently improve overall FM outsourcing
performance services. These concepts might also be applied to other
advanced building assets in other business sectors, such as contemporary
office buildings, airports, hotels and hospitals.
Limitations of the FORT model
However, the concept of the evolution of the outsourcing relationships
types
has its limitation if companies and public bodies have their own subsidiary
property management firms or hire service providers for fixed client-
service
provider relationships at the outset. It is also possible that the pace of FM
practices nationally differ between western and eastern countries. FM is a
relatively new and fast developing profession in the service industry (Hui,
et
al., 2013). The new concept of evolution of outsourcing relationships
between
the FM stakeholders is relatively innovative to the local FM professionals in
the Asian Pacific regions.
36

REFERENCES
Adegoke, B. F. and Adegoke, O. J. (2013) The use of facilities management
in tertiary
institutions in Osun State, Nigeria, Journal of Facilities Management, Vol.
11, No. 2,
pp. 183-192.
Agndal, H. and Nordin, F. (2009) Consequences of outsourcing for
organizational
capabilities: experiences from best practice, Benchmarking: An
International Journal,
Vol. 16, No. 3, pp. 316-34.
Amaratunga, D. and Baldry, D. (1999) Building performance evaluation of

higher
education properties: towards a process model, in Proceedings of the 1999 RICS
COBRA Conference, Salford, UK, Vol. 2, pp.45 – 56.
Baithélemy, J. (2003) The seven deadly sins of outsourcing, Academy of Management
Executive, Vol. 17, No. 2, p. 87 – 98.
Boer, L. D., Gaytan, F. and Arroyo, P. (2006) Case study: A satisficing model of
outsourcing, Supply Chain Management: An International Journal, 11/5, p. 444 – 55.
Boyson, S., Corsi, T. and Rabinovich, E. (1999) Managing effective third party
logistics relationships: what does it take?, Journal of Business Logistics, Vol. 20 No.
1, p. 73-100.
British Standards Institute (2010) Collaborative business relationships: a framework
specification, British Standard 11000-1:2010, British Standards Institute, 31 October.
Brown, J. (2002) Relationship pointers for outsourcing fans, Computing Canada, Vol.
28, Number (23), p6.
Carpentier, V. (2004) Higher Education and the UK Socio-Economic System, Institute
of Education, University of London, London.
Chan, K. (2008) An empirical study of maintenance costs for hotels in Hong Kong,
Journal of Retail and Leisure Property, No. 7, p. 35 – 52.
Chiang, Y. H., Li, J., Choi, N.Y. and Man, K. F. (2013) Evaluating construction
contractors' efficiency in Hong Kong using Data Envelopment Analysis Assurance
Region model, Journal of Facilities Management, Vol. 11, No. 1, pp. 52-68.
Cigolini, R., Miragliotta, G. and Pero, M. (2011) A road-map for outsourcing
facilities-related services in SMEs - Overcome criticalities and build trust, Facilities,
Vol. 29, Number 11/12, p. 445 – 458.

Coenen, C., Felten, D. V. and Schmid, M. (2010) Reputation and public awareness of
facilities management – a quantitative survey, Journal of Facilities Management, Vol.
8, Number 4, p. 256 – 268.
Collis, J. and Hussey, R. (2003), Business Research: A practical guide for
undergraduate and postgraduate students, Second Edition, Palgrave Macmillan.
37
Duyar, I. (2010) Relationship between school facilities conditions and the delivery of
instruction, Journal of Facilities Management, Vol. 8, No. 1, pp. 8-25.
Ferris, J. M. and Graddy, E. (1991) Production cost, transaction costs and local
government contractor choice, Economic Enquiry, Vol. 24, pp. 541-54.
Fianchini, M. (2006) Fitness for purpose: A performance evaluation methodology for
the management of university buildings, Facilities, Vol. 25, No. 3/4, pp. 137-46.
Finch, E. (2012) Facilities Change Management, Wiley – Blackwell, UK.
FM World (2010) Facilities management to benefit from BS 11000, FM World, available
at:www.fm-world.co.uk/news/fm-industry-news/facilities-management-to-benefit-from-bs-
11000 (accessed 18 March 2013).
Fram, S.M. (2010) One built environment: an example for school administrators and
planners, Journal of Educational Administration, Vol. 48, No. 4, pp. 468-89.
Hätönen, J. and Eriksson, T. (2009) 30+ years of research and practice of outsourcing
– Exploring the past and anticipating the future, Journal of International Management, No. 15, p. 142 – 55.
Hamzah, N., Aman, A., Maelah, R., Auzar, S.M. and Amiruddin, R. (2010)
Outsourcing decision processes: a case study of a Malaysian firm, African Journal of
Business Management, Vol. 4 No. 15, p. 3307 - 14.
Harland, C., Knight , L., Lamming , R. and Walker , H. (2005) Outsourcing: assessing

the risks and benefits for organisations, sectors and nations, International Journal of
Operations & Production Management , Vol. 25, Iss. 9/10, p. 831 – 851.
Hui, C. M., Zhang, P. H., and Zheng, X. (2013) Facilities management service and
customer satisfaction in shopping mall sector, Facilities, Vol. 31, No. 5/6, p. 194 –
207.
IAOP (2012) The Global Outsourcing 100, International Association of Outsourcing
Professionals, available at: www.iaop.org (accessed 18 March 2013).
Ikediashi, D. I., Ogunlana, S. O., Boateng, P. and Okwuashi, Onuwa (2012) Analysis
of risks associated with facilities management outsourcing: A multivariate approach,
Journal of Facilities Management, Vol. 10, Number 4, p. 301 – 316.
Ikediashi, D. I., Ogunlana, S. O. and Udo, G. (2013) Structural equation model for
analysing critical risks associated with facilities management outsourcing and its
impact on firm performance, Journal of Facilities Management, Vol. 11, Issue 4.
Insinga, R. C. and Werle, M. J. (2000) Linking outsourcing to business strategy,
Academy of Management Executive, Vol. 14, No. 4, p. 58 – 70.
Jensen, P. A., Voordt, T. V. D., Coenen, C., Felten, D. V., Lindholm, A. L., Nielsen, S.
38
B., Riratanaphong, C. and Pfenninger, M. (2012) In search for the added value of FM:
what we know and what we need to learn, Facilities, Vol. 30, Number 5/6, p. 199 –
217.
Kadefors, A. (2008) Contracting in FM: collaboration, coordination and control,
Journal of Facilities Management, Vol. 6, Number 3, p. 178 – 88.
Kakabadse, N. and Kakabadse, A. (2000) Critical review – outsourcing: a

paradigm
shift, The Journal of Management Development, Vol. 19 No. 8, p. 668-728.
Kakabadse, A. and Kakabadse, N. (2002) Trends in outsourcing: contrasting USA and
Europe, European Management Journal, Vol. 20, No. 2, p. 189–198.
Kavcˇicˇ, K. and Tavcˇar, M. I. (2008) Planning successful partnership in the process
of outsourcing, Kybernetes, Vol. 37, Number 2, p. 241 – 249.
Kishore, R., Rao, H. R., Nam, K., Rajagopalan, S. and Chaudhury, A. (2003) A
Relationship Perspective on IT Outsourcing, Communications of The Association for
Computing Machinery, Vol. 46, No. 12, p. 87 – 92.
Kok, H., Mobach, M. and Omta, S. W. F. (2011) The added value of facility management in the educational environment, Journal of Facilities Management, Vol.
9, No. 4, pp. 249-265.
Kourteli, L. (2000) Scanning the business environment: some conceptual issues,
Benchmarking: An International Journal, Vol. 7, No. 5, p. 406 -13.
Lai, J. and Yik, F. and Jones, P. (2008) Expenditure on operation and maintenance
service and rental income of commercial buildings, Facilities, Vol. 26, No. 5/6, p.242-
265.
Lavy, S. (2008) Facility management practices in higher education buildings: A case
study, Journal of Facilities Management, Vol. 6, No. 4, p. 303-15.
Lee, J-N., Miranda, S. M. and Kim, Y. M. (2004) IT outsourcing strategies: universalistic, contingency, and configurational explanations of success, Information
Systems Research, Vol. 15 No. 2, p. 110-31.
Lehtonen, T. and Salonen, A. (2005) Procurement and relationship management
trends in FM services, paper presented at the IMP Conference, Rotterdam, available
at: www.impgroup.org/uploads/papers/4717.pdf (accessed 15 February 2010).

Li, M. and Choi, T. (2009) Triads in services outsourcing: bridge, bridge decay and
bridge transfer, Journal of Supply Management, Vol. 45 No. 3, p. 27 - 39.
Lok, K. L., Finch, E., Chiang, Y. H. and Chan, C. M. (2010) An Exploratory Model
Linking Facilities Management Outsourcing Performance to Business Performance in
Built Environment, The 1st Greater Pearl River Delta Conference on Building
Operation and Maintenance: Sustainable and Value-for-Money Built Facilities, Hong
Kong, 22 October 2010, p.109 – 18.
    39
Maringe, F. (2006) University and course choice, International Journal of Educational
Management, Vol. 20, No. 6, p. 466-79.
Marshall, D., Lamming, R., Fynes, B. and De Burca, S. (2004) An exploration of the
outsourcing process: a study of the UK telecommunications industry, Proceedings of
the 13th Annual IPSERA Conference, Catania, 4-7 April, p. 554-562.
Maskell, P., Pedersen, T., Petersen, B. and Dick-Nielsen, J. (2005) Learning paths to
offshore outsourcing – from cost reduction to knowledge seeking. DRUID Working
Paper, vol. 05–17. Available at World Wide Web bURL:http://www.druid.dkN.
Moore, M. and Finch, E. (2004) Facilities Management in South East Asia, Facilities,
Vol. 22, No. 9/10, p, 259 - 70.
Plane, C. V. and Green, A. N. (2012) Buyer-supplier collaboration: the aim of FM
procurement?, Facilities, Vol. 30, Number 3/4, p.152 – 163.
Price, I.F., Matzdorf, F., Smith, I. and Aghai, H. (2003) The impact of facilities on
student choice of university, Facilities, Vol. 21, No. 10, p. 212-30.
Remenyi, D., Williams, B., Money, A. and Swartz, E. (1998) Doing Research in

Business and Management: An Introduction to Process and Method' SAGE
Publications. London.
Reynolds, G.L. and Cain, D. (2006) Final Report on the Impact of Facilities on the
Recruitment and Retention of Students, Center for Facilities Research, APPA,
Alexandria, Virginia.
Sabherwal, R. (1999) The role of trust in outsourced IS development projects,
Commun, 42, 2, Feb, 80 – 6.
Saunders, M., Lewis, P. and Thornhill, A. (2003) Research Methods for Business
Students, Third Edition, Prentice Hall.
Sia, S. K., Koh, C. and Tan, C. X. (2008) Strategic Maneuvers for Outsourcing
Flexibility: An Empirical Assessment, Decision Sciences, Vol. 39, No. 3, p. 407 – 43.
Tanner, C.K. (2009) Effects of school design on students outcomes, Journal of
Educational Administration, Vol. 47, No. 3, p. 381-99.
Tertiary Education Facilities Management Association (2011) 2010 Benchmark
Report, Tertiary Education Facilities Management Association (TEFMA) Incorporated, Australia.
Univeristies UK (2009) Higher Education Pay and Prices Index (HEPPI), Univeristies UK, London.
University Grants Committee (2010) Aspirations for the Higher Education System in
Hong Kong: Report of the University Grants Committee, December, University
40
Grants Committee.
Vidalakis, C., Sun, M. and Papa, A. (2013) The quality and value of higher education
facilities: a comparative study, Facilities, Vol. 31, Issue 11/12.
Williamson, O.E. (1981) The economics of organisation: The transaction cost

approach, Amer. J, Sociology, 87, 3, 548 - 77.

Yik, F. and Lai, J. (2005) The trend of outsourcing for building services operation and

maintenance in Hong Kong, Facilities, Vol. 23, No. 1/2, p. 63-72.

Yin, R. (2003) Case Study Research: Design and Methods,

Discussion and Conclusion

Understanding on FM outsourcing relationships in Higher Education Sector
The analysis of the simultaneous relationships between FM outsourcing
relationship types and dimensions (substitution of ownership, substitution
of
control, competitive position and long-term planning) enhances the overall
understanding of FM outsourcing relationships. The empirical investigation
reveals a significant relationship between FM outsourcing relationship
types
and services in the context of Hong Kong's higher education sector. Clients
and service providers have indicated that applying the FM outsourcing
    relationship types improves the quality of the services. Meanwhile, the
results
of the hypotheses testing indicate that FM outsourcing relationship types
are
used in related services; that is, the outsourcing categories of a specific FM
outsourcing contract will be achieved through prediction at the level of
substitution of ownership, substitution of control, competitive positions
and
long-term planning.

    Importantly, this research establishes a link between 'high quality FM
outsourcing service' and potential increases in substitution of ownership,
substitution of control, competitive positions and long-term planning. The
relationship between FM outsourcing relationship types and service is
statistically significant. The majority of previous FM outsourcing studies
has
discussed the causes of service providers' substandard outsourcing

performance without considering the relationships among the four FM outsourcing relationship dimensions in FM outsourcing contracts. This research investigates these relationships from both the clients and the service

providers' perspectives, with regard to FM outsourcing relationship categories

and services.

   - Future research directions

Although the focus of this study is the importance of FM outsourcing relationship types and dimensions in Hong Kong's higher education sector, and their centrality has been confirmed, the researcher believes that the demand and supply of FM services will play a major role in the future of the higher education industry. As previously noted, universities' financial costs have recently increased, which means that the FM client-strategists must plan

updated FM strategies to solve the current and future financial problems. As a

result, further research is required to explore the relationships among critical

FM outsourcing contracts.

   Finally, it is not possible for any single study to cover every aspect of a topic,

and this study is no exception. The 'evolution and revolution' of FM outsourcing relationship types and dimensions will continue, and thus the topic deserves further investigation. For instance, it is important to investigate

how clients and service providers can manage the financial aspects of FM outsourcing contracts to efficiently improve overall FM outsourcing performance services. These concepts might also be applied to other advanced building assets in other business sectors, such as contemporary office buildings, airports, hotels and hospitals.

Limitations of the FORT model

However, the concept of the evolution of the outsourcing relationships types

has its limitation if companies and public bodies have their own subsidiary property management firms or hire service providers for fixed client-service

provider relationships at the outset. It is also possible that the pace of FM practices nationally differ between western and eastern countries. FM is a relatively new and fast developing profession in the service industry (Hui, et

al., 2013). The new concept of evolution of outsourcing relationships between

the FM stakeholders is relatively innovative to the local FM professionals in the Asian Pacific regions.

REFERENCES

Adegoke, B. F. and Adegoke, O. J. (2013) The use of facilities management in tertiary

institutions in Osun State, Nigeria, Journal of Facilities Management, Vol. 11, No. 2,

pp. 183-192.

Agndal, H. and Nordin, F. (2009) Consequences of outsourcing for organizational

capabilities: experiences from best practice, Benchmarking: An International Journal,

Vol. 16, No. 3, pp. 316-34.

Amaratunga, D. and Baldry, D. (1999) Building performance evaluation of higher

education properties: towards a process model, in Proceedings of the 1999 RICS

COBRA Conference, Salford, UK, Vol. 2, pp.45 – 56.

Baithélemy, J. (2003) The seven deadly sins of outsourcing, Academy of Management

Executive, Vol. 17, No. 2, p. 87 – 98.

Boer, L. D., Gaytan, F. and Arroyo, P. (2006) Case study: A satisficing model of

outsourcing, Supply Chain Management: An International Journal, 11/5, p. 444 – 55.

Boyson, S., Corsi, T. and Rabinovich, E. (1999) Managing effective third party

logistics relationships: what does it take?, Journal of Business Logistics, Vol. 20 No.

1, p. 73-100.

British Standards Institute (2010) Collaborative business relationships: a framework specification, British Standard 11000-1:2010, British Standards Institute, 31 October.

Brown, J. (2002) Relationship pointers for outsourcing fans, Computing Canada, Vol.

28, Number (23), p6.

Carpentier, V. (2004) Higher Education and the UK Socio-Economic System, Institute

of Education, University of London, London.

Chan, K. (2008) An empirical study of maintenance costs for hotels in Hong Kong,

Journal of Retail and Leisure Property, No. 7, p. 35 – 52.

Chiang, Y. H., Li, J., Choi, N.Y. and Man, K. F. (2013) Evaluating construction

contractors' efficiency in Hong Kong using Data Envelopment Analysis Assurance

Region model, Journal of Facilities Management, Vol. 11, No. 1, pp. 52-68.

Cigolini, R., Miragliotta, G. and Pero, M. (2011) A road-map for outsourcing facilities-related services in SMEs - Overcome criticalities and build trust, Facilities,

Vol. 29, Number 11/12, p. 445 – 458.

Coenen, C., Felten, D. V. and Schmid, M. (2010) Reputation and public awareness of

facilities management – a quantitative survey, Journal of Facilities Management, Vol.

8, Number 4, p. 256 – 268.

Collis, J. and Hussey, R. (2003), Business Research: A practical guide for

undergraduate and postgraduate students, Second Edition, Palgrave Macmillan.

37

Duyar, I. (2010) Relationship between school facilities conditions and the delivery of

instruction, Journal of Facilities Management, Vol. 8, No. 1, pp. 8-25.

Ferris, J. M. and Graddy, E. (1991) Production cost, transaction costs and local

government contractor choice, Economic Enquiry, Vol. 24, pp. 541-54.

Fianchini, M. (2006) Fitness for purpose: A performance evaluation methodology for

the management of university buildings, Facilities, Vol. 25, No. 3/4, pp.

137-46.

Finch, E. (2012) Facilities Change Management, Wiley – Blackwell, UK.

FM World (2010) Facilities management to benefit from BS 11000, FM World, available

at:www.fm-world.co.uk/news/fm-industry-news/facilities-management-to-benefit-from-bs-

11000 (accessed 18 March 2013).

Fram, S.M. (2010) One built environment: an example for school administrators and

planners, Journal of Educational Administration, Vol. 48, No. 4, pp. 468-89.

Hätönen, J. and Eriksson, T. (2009) 30+ years of research and practice of outsourcing

– Exploring the past and anticipating the future, Journal of International Management, No. 15, p. 142 – 55.

Hamzah, N., Aman, A., Maelah, R., Auzar, S.M. and Amiruddin, R. (2010) Outsourcing decision processes: a case study of a Malaysian firm, African Journal of

Business Management, Vol. 4 No. 15, p. 3307 - 14.

Harland, C., Knight , L., Lamming , R. and Walker , H. (2005) Outsourcing: assessing

the risks and benefits for organisations, sectors and nations, International Journal of

Operations & Production Management , Vol. 25, Iss. 9/10, p. 831 – 851.

Hui, C. M., Zhang, P. H., and Zheng, X. (2013) Facilities management service and

customer satisfaction in shopping mall sector, Facilities, Vol. 31, No. 5/6, p. 194 –

207.

IAOP (2012) The Global Outsourcing 100, International Association of Outsourcing

Professionals, available at: www.iaop.org (accessed 18 March 2013).

Ikediashi, D. I., Ogunlana, S. O., Boateng, P. and Okwuashi, Onuwa (2012) Analysis

of risks associated with facilities management outsourcing: A multivariate approach,

Journal of Facilities Management, Vol. 10, Number 4, p. 301 – 316.

Ikediashi, D. I., Ogunlana, S. O. and Udo, G. (2013) Structural equation model for

analysing critical risks associated with facilities management outsourcing and its

impact on firm performance, Journal of Facilities Management, Vol. 11, Issue 4.

Insinga, R. C. and Werle, M. J. (2000) Linking outsourcing to business strategy,

Academy of Management Executive, Vol. 14, No. 4, p. 58 – 70.

Jensen, P. A., Voordt, T. V. D., Coenen, C., Felten, D. V., Lindholm, A. L., Nielsen, S.

   38

B., Riratanaphong, C. and Pfenninger, M. (2012) In search for the added value of FM:

what we know and what we need to learn, Facilities, Vol. 30, Number 5/6, p. 199 –

217.

Kadefors, A. (2008) Contracting in FM: collaboration, coordination and control,

Journal of Facilities Management, Vol. 6, Number 3, p. 178 – 88.

Kakabadse, N. and Kakabadse, A. (2000) Critical review – outsourcing: a paradigm

shift, The Journal of Management Development, Vol. 19 No. 8, p. 668-728.

Kakabadse, A. and Kakabadse, N. (2002) Trends in outsourcing: contrasting USA and

Europe, European Management Journal, Vol. 20, No. 2, p. 189–198.

Kavcˇicˇ, K. and Tavcˇar, M. I. (2008) Planning successful partnership in the process

of outsourcing, Kybernetes, Vol. 37, Number 2, p. 241 – 249.

Kishore, R., Rao, H. R., Nam, K., Rajagopalan, S. and Chaudhury, A. (2003) A

Relationship Perspective on IT Outsourcing, Communications of The Association for

Computing Machinery, Vol. 46, No. 12, p. 87 – 92.

Kok, H., Mobach, M. and Omta, S. W. F. (2011) The added value of facility management in the educational environment, Journal of Facilities Management, Vol.

9, No. 4, pp. 249-265.

Kourteli, L. (2000) Scanning the business environment: some conceptual

issues,
Benchmarking: An International Journal, Vol. 7, No. 5, p. 406 -13.
Lai, J. and Yik, F. and Jones, P. (2008) Expenditure on operation and maintenance
service and rental income of commercial buildings, Facilities, Vol. 26, No. 5/6, p.242-
265.
Lavy, S. (2008) Facility management practices in higher education buildings: A case
study, Journal of Facilities Management, Vol. 6, No. 4, p. 303-15.
Lee, J-N., Miranda, S. M. and Kim, Y. M. (2004) IT outsourcing strategies:
universalistic, contingency, and configurational explanations of success, Information
Systems Research, Vol. 15 No. 2, p. 110-31.
Lehtonen, T. and Salonen, A. (2005) Procurement and relationship management
trends in FM services, paper presented at the IMP Conference, Rotterdam, available
at: www.impgroup.org/uploads/papers/4717.pdf (accessed 15 February 2010).
Li, M. and Choi, T. (2009) Triads in services outsourcing: bridge, bridge decay and
bridge transfer, Journal of Supply Management, Vol. 45 No. 3, p. 27 - 39.
Lok, K. L., Finch, E., Chiang, Y. H. and Chan, C. M. (2010) An Exploratory Model
Linking Facilities Management Outsourcing Performance to Business Performance in
Built Environment, The 1st Greater Pearl River Delta Conference on Building
Operation and Maintenance: Sustainable and Value-for-Money Built Facilities, Hong
Kong, 22 October 2010, p.109 – 18.
39
Maringe, F. (2006) University and course choice, International Journal of Educational
Management, Vol. 20, No. 6, p. 466-79.
Marshall, D., Lamming, R., Fynes, B. and De Burca, S. (2004) An exploration of the

outsourcing process: a study of the UK telecommunications industry, Proceedings of
the 13th Annual IPSERA Conference, Catania, 4-7 April, p. 554-562.
Maskell, P., Pedersen, T., Petersen, B. and Dick-Nielsen, J. (2005) Learning paths to
offshore outsourcing – from cost reduction to knowledge seeking. DRUID Working
Paper, vol. 05–17. Available at World Wide Web bURL:http://www.druid.dkN.
Moore, M. and Finch, E. (2004) Facilities Management in South East Asia, Facilities,
Vol. 22, No. 9/10, p, 259 - 70.
Plane, C. V. and Green, A. N. (2012) Buyer-supplier collaboration: the aim of FM
procurement?, Facilities, Vol. 30, Number 3/4, p.152 – 163.
Price, I.F., Matzdorf, F., Smith, I. and Aghai, H. (2003) The impact of facilities on
student choice of university, Facilities, Vol. 21, No. 10, p. 212-30.
Remenyi, D., Williams, B., Money, A. and Swartz, E. (1998) Doing Research in
Business and Management: An Introduction to Process and Method' SAGE
Publications. London.
Reynolds, G.L. and Cain, D. (2006) Final Report on the Impact of Facilities on the
Recruitment and Retention of Students, Center for Facilities Research, APPA,
Alexandria, Virginia.
Sabherwal, R. (1999) The role of trust in outsourced IS development projects,
Commun, 42, 2, Feb, 80 – 6.
Saunders, M., Lewis, P. and Thornhill, A. (2003) Research Methods for Business
Students, Third Edition, Prentice Hall.
Sia, S. K., Koh, C. and Tan, C. X. (2008) Strategic Maneuvers for Outsourcing
Flexibility: An Empirical Assessment, Decision Sciences, Vol. 39, No. 3, p. 407 – 43.

Tanner, C.K. (2009) Effects of school design on students outcomes, Journal of
Educational Administration, Vol. 47, No. 3, p. 381-99.
Tertiary Education Facilities Management Association (2011) 2010 Benchmark
Report, Tertiary Education Facilities Management Association (TEFMA)
Incorporated, Australia.
Univeristies UK (2009) Higher Education Pay and Prices Index (HEPPI),
Univeristies UK, London.
University Grants Committee (2010) Aspirations for the Higher Education System in
Hong Kong: Report of the University Grants Committee, December, University
40
Grants Committee.
Vidalakis, C., Sun, M. and Papa, A. (2013) The quality and value of higher education
facilities: a comparative study, Facilities, Vol. 31, Issue 11/12.
Williamson, O.E. (1981) The economics of organisation: The transaction cost
approach, Amer. J, Sociology, 87, 3, 548 - 77.
Yik, F. and Lai, J. (2005) The trend of outsourcing for building services operation and
maintenance in Hong Kong, Facilities, Vol. 23, No. 1/2, p. 63-72.
Yin, R. (2003) Case Study Research: Design and Methods,

Keywords Client satisfaction, Outsourcing arrangements, Outsourcing relationships, Outsourcing services, Performance of service providers, Strategic manoeuvres Paper type Research paper Introduction Although the construction industry has long been a powerful engines

Reference

References Adegoke, B.F. and Adegoke, O.J. (2013), "The use of facilities management in tertiary institutions in Osun State, Nigeria", Journal of Facilities Management, Vol. 11 No. 2, pp. 183-192.

Agndal, H. and Nordin, F. (2009), "Consequences of outsourcing for organizational capabilities: experiences from best practice", Benchmarking: An International Journal, Vol. 16 No. 3, pp. 316-334.

Amaratunga, D. and Baldry, D. (1999), "Building performance evaluation of higher education properties: towards a process model", Proceedings of the 1999 RICS COBRA Conference, Salford, Vol. 2, pp. 45-56. Baithélemy, J. (2003),

"The seven deadly sins of outsourcing", Academy of Management Executive, Vol. 17 No. 2, pp. 87-98.

Baithélemy, J. (2003), "The seven deadly sins of outsourcing", Academy of Management Executive, Vol. 17 No. 2, pp. 87-98. Blau, P.M. (1964), Exchange and Power in Social Life, Wiley, New York, NY. Boyson, S., Corsi, T. and Rabinovich, E. (1999), "Managing effective third party logistics relationships: what does it take?", Journal of Business Logistics, Vol. 20 No. 1, pp. 73-100.

British Standards Institute (2010), Collaborative Business Relationships: A Framework Specification, British Standard 11000-1:2010, British Standards Institute, London, 31 October.

Brown, J. (2002), "Relationship pointers for outsourcing fans", Computing Canada, Vol. 28 No. 23, p. 6. Carpentier, V. (2004), Higher Education and the UK Socio-Economic System, Institute of Education, University of London, London. Chan, K. (2008), "An empirical study of maintenance costs for hotels in Hong Kong", Journal of Retail and Leisure Property, Vol. 7 No. 1, pp. 35-52. Chiang, Y.H., Li, J., Choi, N.Y. and Man, K.F. (2013), "Evaluating construction contractors' efficiency in Hong Kong using Data Envelopment Analysis Assurance Region model", Journal of Facilities Management, Vol. 11 No. 1, pp. 52-68.

Cigolini, R., Miragliotta, G. and Pero, M. (2011), "A road-map for outsourcing facilities-related services in SMEs – overcome criticalities and build trust", Facilities, Vol. 29 Nos 11/12, pp. 445-458.

Coenen, C., Felten, D.V. and Schmid, M. (2010), "Reputation and public awareness of facilities management – a quantitative survey", Journal of

Facilities Management, Vol. 8 No. 4, pp. 256-268.

Collis, J. and Hussey, R. (2003), Business Research: A Practical Guide for Undergraduate and Postgraduate Students, Second Edition, Palgrave Macmillan, London. Duyar, I. (2010), "Relationship between school facilities conditions and the delivery of instruction", Journal of Facilities Management, Vol. 8 No. 1, pp. 8-25.

Ferris, J.M. and Graddy, E. (1991), "Production cost, transaction costs and local government contractor choice", Economic Enquiry, Vol. 24 No. 3, pp. 541-554. Fianchini, M. (2006), "Fitness for purpose: a performance evaluation methodology for the management of university buildings", Facilities, Vol. 25 Nos 3/4, pp. 137-146. Finch, E. (2012), Facilities Change Management, Wiley – Blackwell, London. 845

Facilities management outsourcing relationships Downloaded by HONG KONG INSTITUTE OF VOCATIONAL EDUCATION At 03:15 25 October 2015 (PT) FM World (2010), "Facilities management to benefit from BS 11000", FM World, available at: www.fm-world.co.uk/news/fm-industry-news/facilities-management-to-benefit-from-bs11000 (accessed 18 March 2013).

Fram, S.M. (2010), "One built environment: an example for school administrators and planners", Journal of Educational Administration, Vol. 48 No. 4, pp. 468-489. Hamzah, N., Aman, A., Maelah, R., Auzar, S.M. and Amiruddin, R. (2010), "Outsourcing decision processes: a case study of a Malaysian firm", African Journal of Business Management, Vol. 4 No. 15, pp. 3307-3314.

Harland, C., Knight, L., Lamming, R. and Walker, H. (2005), "Outsourcing: assessing the risks and benefits for organisations, sectors and nations", International Journal of Operations & Production Management, Vol. 25 Nos 9/10, pp. 831-851. Hätönen, J. and Eriksson, T. (2009), "30 years of research and practice of outsourcing – exploring the past and anticipating the future", Journal of International Management, Vol. 15 No. 2, pp. 142-155. Hui, C.M., Zhang, P.H. and Zheng, X. (2013), "Facilities management service and customer satisfaction in shopping mall sector", Facilities, Vol. 31 Nos 5/6, pp. 194-207. IAOP (2012), "The global outsourcing 100", International Association of Outsourcing Professionals, available at: www.iaop.org (accessed 18 March 2013).

Ikediashi, D.I., Ogunlana, S.O., Boateng, P. and Okwuashi, Onuwa (2012), "Analysis of risks associated with facilities management outsourcing: a multivariate approach", Journal of Facilities Management,

Vol. 10 No. 4, pp. 301-316.

Ikediashi, D.I., Ogunlana, S.O. and Udo, G. (2013), "Structural equation model for analysing critical risks associated with facilities management outsourcing and its impact on firm performance", Journal of Facilities Management, Vol. 11 No. 4. Insinga, R.C. and Werle, M.J. (2000), "Linking outsourcing to business strategy", Academy of Management Executive, Vol. 14 No. 4, pp. 58-70. Jensen, M.C. and Meckling, W.H. (1976), "Theory of the firm: managerial behavior, agency costs, and ownership structure", Journal of Financial Economics, Vol. 3 No. 1, pp. 305-360.

Jensen, P.A., Voordt, T.V.D., Coenen, C., Felten, D.V., Lindholm, A.L., Nielsen, S.B., Riratanaphong, C. and Pfenninger, M. (2012), "In search for the added value of FM: what we know and what we need to learn", Facilities, Vol. 30 Nos 5/6, pp. 199-217. Kadefors, A. (2008), "Contracting in FM: collaboration, coordination and control", Journal of Facilities Management, Vol. 6 No. 3, pp. 178-188. Kakabadse, A. and Kakabadse, N. (2002), "Trends in outsourcing: contrasting USA and Europe", European Management Journal, Vol. 20 No. 2, pp. 189-198.

Kakabadse, N. and Kakabadse, A. (2000), "Critical review – outsourcing: a paradigm shift", The Journal of Management Development, Vol. 19 No. 8, pp. 668-728. Kavčič, K. and Tavčar, M.I. (2008), "Planning successful partnership in the process of outsourcing", Kybernetes, Vol. 37 No. 2, pp. 241-249.

Kishore, R., Rao, H.R., Nam, K., Rajagopalan, S. and Chaudhury, A. (2003), "A relationship perspective on IT outsourcing", Communications of The Association for Computing Machinery, Vol. 46 No. 12, pp. 87-92.

Kok, H., Mobach, M. and Omta, S.W.F. (2011), "The added value of facility management in the educational environment", Journal of Facilities Management, Vol. 9 No. 4, pp. 249-265. Kourteli, L. (2000), "Scanning the business environment: some conceptual issues", Benchmarking: An International Journal, Vol. 7 No. 5, pp. 406-413. F 33,13/14 846 Downloaded by HONG KONG INSTITUTE OF VOCATIONAL EDUCATION At 03:15 25 October 2015 (PT) Lai, J. and Yik, F. and Jones, P. (2008), "Expenditure on operation and maintenance service and rental income of commercial buildings", Facilities, Vol. 26 Nos 5/6, pp. 242-265.

Lavy, S. (2008), "Facility management practices in higher education buildings: a case study", Journal of Facilities Management, Vol. 6 No. 4, pp. 303-315. Lee, J.N., Miranda, S.M. and Kim, Y.M. (2004), "IT outsourcing strategies: universalistic, contingency, and configurational explanations of success", Information Systems Research, Vol. 15 No. 2, pp. 110-131.

Lehtonen, T. and Salonen, A. (2005), "Procurement and relationship management trends in FM services", paper presented at the IMP Conference, Rotterdam, available at: www.impgroup. org/uploads/papers/ 4717.pdf (accessed 15 February 2010).

Li, M. and Choi, T. (2009), "Triads in services outsourcing: bridge, bridge decay and bridge transfer", Journal of Supply Management, Vol. 45 No. 3, pp. 27-39. Lok, K.L. and Finch, E. (2012), "A contingency model for outsourcing relationships in the facilities sector", paper presented at the WWP Conference, Texas, available at: http://ifma.confex. com/ifma/ ww2012/webprogram/Session2839.html (accessed 18 March 2013).

Lok, K.L., Finch, E., Chiang, Y.H. and Chan, C.M. (2010), "An exploratory model linking facilities management outsourcing performance to business performance in built environment", The 1st Greater Pearl River Delta Conference on Building Operation and Maintenance: Sustainable and Value-for-Money Built Facilities, Macau, 22 October, pp. 109-118.

Maringe, F. (2006), "University and course choice", International Journal of Educational Management, Vol. 20 No. 6, pp. 466-479.

Marshall, D., Lamming, R., Fynes, B. and De Burca, S. (2004), "An exploration of the outsourcing process: a study of the UK telecommunications industry", Proceedings of the 13th Annual IPSERA Conference, Catania, 4-7 April, pp. 554-562. Maskell, P., Pedersen, T., Petersen, B. and Dick-Nielsen, J. (2005), "Learning paths to offshore outsourcing – from cost reduction to knowledge seeking", DRUID Working Paper, Vols 05/17, available at: www.druid.dkN Moore, M. and Finch, E. (2004), "Facilities management in South East Asia", Facilities, Vol. 22 Nos 9/10, pp. 259-270.

Pfeffer, J. and Salancik, G. (1978), The External Control of Organizations, Harper & Row, New York, NY. Plane, C.V. and Green, A.N. (2012), "Buyer-supplier collaboration: the aim of FM procurement?", Facilities, Vol. 30 Nos 3/4, pp. 152-163. Price, I.F., Matzdorf, F., Smith, I. and Aghai, H. (2003), "The impact of facilities on student choice of university", Facilities, Vol. 21 No. 10, pp. 212-230.

Remenyi, D., Williams, B., Money, A. and Swartz, E. (1998), Doing Research in Business and Management: An Introduction to Process and Method', Sage Publications, London. Reynolds, G.L. and Cain, D. (2006), Final Report on the Impact of Facilities on the Recruitment and Retention of Students, Center for Facilities Research, APPA, Alexandria, VA.

Sabherwal, R. (1999), "The role of trust in outsourced IS development projects", Commun, Vol. 42 No. 2, pp. 80-86.

Saunders, M., Lewis, P. and Thornhill, A. (2003), Research Methods for Business Students, Third Edition, Prentice Hall, Upper Saddle River, New Jersey. Schumpeter, J.A. (1936), The Theory of Economic Development, Cambridge University Press, Cambridge. 847 Facilities management outsourcing relationships Downloaded by HONG KONG INSTITUTE OF VOCATIONAL EDUCATION At 03:15 25 October 2015 (PT) Sia, S.K., Koh, C. and Tan, C.X. (2008), "Strategic maneuvers for outsourcing flexibility: an empirical assessment", Decision Sciences, Vol. 39 No. 3, pp. 407-443.

Tanner, C.K. (2009), "Effects of school design on students outcomes", Journal of Educational Administration, Vol. 47 No. 3, pp. 381-399. Universities, U.K. (2009), Higher Education Pay and Prices Index (HEPPI), Univeristies UK, London. University Grants Committee (2010), "Aspirations for the higher education system in Hong Kong: report of the University Grants Committee", University Grants Committee, Hong Kong, December. Vidalakis, C., Sun, M. and Papa, A. (2013), "The quality and value of higher education facilities: a comparative study", Facilities, Vol. 31 Nos 11/12. Williamson, O.E. (1981), "The economics of organisation: the transaction cost approach", American Journal of Sociology, Vol. 87 No. 3, pp. 548-577. Yik, F. and Lai, J. (2005), "The trend of outsourcing for building services operation and maintenance in Hong Kong", Facilities, Vol. 23 Nos 1/2, pp. 63-72. Yin, R. (2003), Case Study Research: Design and Methods, 3rd ed., Sage Publications, Thousand Oaks.

Corresponding author Ka Leung Lok can be contacted at: k.l.lok@edu.salford.ac.uk

www.ingramcontent.com/pod-product-compliance
Lightning Source LLC
Chambersburg PA
CBHW052205150726
48002CB00003B/1126